Ava's Voice

Written by Lisa Rajan
Illustrated by Alejandra Ruiz

Collins

Chapter 1

It was Monday morning and everybody in Shona's class was chattering about what they had done at the weekend.

Otis was telling everyone that he had been swimming. Shona heard Vishal and Stanley laughing about a giant flying chicken in a film they had watched together.

Sofia told Shona that she had helped her mum paint the kitchen. Jasmine gave Bobby a bracelet that she had made.

Shona noticed that the only person who wasn't talking was Ava, the new girl.

Otis showed Ava a badge with a swimmer on it.

"I brought this in for show and tell," he told her proudly. "I swam two lengths of the pool without stopping or touching the wall at the side. I can swim front crawl and backstroke. Can you?"

Ava's face froze.

"Backstroke is my favourite," continued Otis. "What's yours?"

Ava didn't move.

I wonder why Ava ignored Otis, thought Shona.

Otis shrugged and went to find someone else to show his swimming badge to.

Mr McAlister waited until everyone had taken their seats.

"It's friendship week," he told the class. "I want you all to get into groups of five and think of activities we could do to celebrate our friendships. Now, if there are 30 of you in the class, how many groups of five will that be?"

Half the class put their hands up.

"Ava?" encouraged Mr McAlister gently. "Do you know the answer?"

Ava stared blankly. She didn't speak.

Maybe Ava didn't understand the question, thought Shona.

"Six!" shouted Bobby.

Chapter 2

Shona made a group with Jasmine, Sofia, Bobby and Ava.

"What about decorating the new buddy bench?" suggested Sofia.

"I don't like drawing," said Bobby.

"What about making friendship bracelets?" suggested Shona, pointing at Bobby's wrist.

"Oh yes!" said Jasmine. "Shall I make one for you, Ava? Then we would be friends."

Ava didn't reply.
Shona was surprised.

Doesn't Ava want new friends? wondered Shona. *She has only played with Lila since she started at our school. I wonder why she hasn't played with anyone else?*

Mr McAlister came to hear their ideas. Shona told him that her group wanted to make friendship bracelets.

"We didn't all agree on that idea," protested Sofia.

"No, but it was three to one…" said Shona.
"Bobby, Jasmine and me against you, Sofia."

"But Ava is on my side," claimed Sofia.
"She wants to decorate the buddy bench.
She is just feeling too shy to say anything."

Everyone looked at Ava. Her face flushed red.

Maybe Sofia is right, wondered Shona. *Maybe Ava is feeling shy.*

Chapter 3

At break time, Vishal and Stanley were playing 'Would You Rather' in the playground.

"Would you rather fight a chicken the size of a dragon or a dragon the size of a chicken?" Vishal asked Stanley.

"A chicken-sized dragon!" laughed Stanley.

"What about you, Ava?" Vishal called over to her. "Which would you rather fight?"

Ava didn't answer his question. She didn't even look in his direction.

Maybe Ava couldn't hear Vishal, thought Shona. *Perhaps there is something wrong with her hearing?*

Shona spotted Lila near the buddy bench.

"You're friends with Ava the new girl, aren't you?" Shona asked Lila.

"Yes, I've known her since I was two years old," replied Lila. "She lives next door to me."

"Has she always been quiet?" asked Shona. "Does she find it hard to listen?"

"I don't think so," said Lila.

"Then why doesn't she talk?" asked Shona, curiously.

Lila looked confused. "What do you mean, Shona?" she said.

"I have never heard her say anything," said Shona. "Have you?"

"Yes she talks to me fine," said Lila.

"Even at school?" asked Shona.

"When it's just us playing together," said Lila. "Does it matter?"

Lila skipped off to go and play. She found Ava on the climbing frame.

They turned cartwheels together. They pretended the floor was lava. They rescued each other from sharks.

Mr McAlister wandered over to the buddy bench.

"Are you alright?" he asked Shona.

"Yes," said Shona. "I was just thinking about Ava. She ignored Otis. She didn't reply to Vishal. She didn't put her hand up when you asked us that sum. She didn't choose a friendship activity. I know I haven't played with her or been in a group with her before today, but now that I think about it, I haven't heard her say a single word since the beginning of term," Shona said sadly. "Lila says that Ava can talk, but that's just Lila."

Chapter 4

At home time, Shona climbed the net of the climbing frame as she waited for her mum to collect her.

She heard a voice that she hadn't heard before.

"Daddy! Daddy!"

It was Ava! Shona was so surprised, her foot slipped through one of the holes.

Ava ran over to her dad. She flung her arms towards him and he lifted her up into the air.

Mr McAlister signalled to Ava's dad across the playground.

Ava's dad put her down and walked over to Mr McAlister's classroom. They chatted for a short while.

"Would it be alright to tell the children about Ava?" asked Mr McAlister.

Ava's dad nodded, "I think that's a good idea."

Ava went to fetch her bag.

"Help! I'm stuck!" yelped Shona, waving frantically from the climbing frame.

Ava hesitated, but there was no one else around who could help. She ran over and reached up to help Shona free her foot.

"Thanks, Ava! Now I had better help you, or the sharks will get us both!" said Shona, hoisting Ava up onto the platform.

Chapter 5

The next morning, Mr McAlister found Shona in the playground.

"Do you remember telling me your worries about Ava yesterday?" he asked her.

"Yes," said Shona.

"Well, Ava has something called selective mutism," said Mr McAlister. "It means that she sometimes finds it difficult to talk, especially with new people or in a new situation."

"Like starting a new school?" asked Shona.

"Yes," said Mr McAlister. "And it's harder when she feels under pressure to talk or if there is lots of attention on her."

"Ava finds it easier if there is a game or activity to focus on instead," said Mr McAlister.

"Like escaping from sharks?" asked Shona.

"Yes," laughed Mr McAlister.

"Or climbing the rigging?" smiled Shona.
"Ava is very good at that!"

"My dad was going to take me to the climbing wall on Saturday," Shona told Mr McAlister. "I think I will ask him to ask Ava's dad if she would like to come with us. We could invite Lila as well and make it a triple playdate!"

Shona spotted Ava and Lila decorating the buddy bench. She ran over to join them.

Ava was drawing a dragon the size of a chicken.

Lila was drawing a chicken the size of a dragon.

"Are they fighting?" asked Shona.

"No … they are both trying to escape from the sharks," said Lila.

Shona took a pen from the pot.

"They are going to need a pirate ship then, aren't they?" she grinned. "I hope they can climb the rigging as well as Ava can!"

When does Ava feel pressure to talk?

Ideas for reading

Written by Gill Matthews
Primary Literacy Consultant

Reading objectives:
- discuss and clarify the meanings of words, linking new meanings to known vocabulary
- make inferences on the basis of what is being said and done
- answer and ask questions

Spoken language objectives:
- use relevant strategies to build their vocabulary
- articulate and justify answers, arguments and opinions
- participate in discussions, presentations, performances, role play, improvisations and debates

Curriculum links: Relationships education: Caring friendships

Interest words: suggested, protested, claimed, yelped

Word count: 1196

Build a context for reading
- Ask children to look at the front cover and to read the title.
- Explore what they think the book might be about.
- Read the back cover blurb and explore children's ideas as to why Ava hasn't spoken at school, being sensitive of their own experiences.

Understand and apply reading strategies
- Read pp2–7 aloud, using meaning, punctuation and dialogue to read with appropriate expression.
- Ask children what they think about Ava. Encourage them to support their responses with reasons and evidence from the text.
- Give children the opportunity to read the rest of the book, pausing after each chapter to discuss the character of Ava.
- Discuss why they think Ava will only talk to Lila.